The

Masculine

Club

How to Never Run Out of Things to Say - Verbal Game, Storytelling and Flirting.

Jeremy Gaines

Table of Content

Introduction

Historically, it's been a complex blend of strength, leadership, protection, and emotional resilience qualities traditionally admired and encouraged in men.

The concept of masculinity often finds itself under a microscope, sometimes celebrated, other times critiqued. But what exactly is masculinity? Historically, it's been a complex blend of strength, leadership, protection, and emotional resilience qualities traditionally admired and encouraged in men. But how did this begin, and more importantly, how does it fit into our current society, especially in interactions with others, including women?

Let's journey back to the roots. In ancient times, masculinity was straightforward men were hunters, gatherers, and protectors. Their role was defined by physical strength and stoicism, qualities essential for survival. But haven't we evolved past that? Yes, and no. While the physical demands of ancient times have diminished, the underlying qualities strength, leadership, and resilience remain crucial, albeit in more nuanced forms.

So, why is there a growing emphasis on developing a strong masculine drive in today's world, particularly in dealing with people, and specifically women? Haven't we moved beyond gender stereotypes? The answer is both yes and no. We have progressed, but the core qualities of masculinity still hold significant value. They just need to be applied wisely and respectfully.

But what kind of strength are we talking about here? Not the brute physical strength of our ancestors, but strength of character. This means being reliable, dependable, and having the courage to stand up for what is right. Isn't that something everyone, regardless of gender, finds attractive and reassuring?

Leadership, another key masculine trait, isn't about dominance or control. It's about guidance, making decisions with confidence and consideration. In a relationship, for instance, this could mean taking the initiative in planning a date or calmly handling a crisis. Doesn't this kind of leadership foster a sense of security and partnership?

The Masculine Club is a concise and compelling guide designed for the modern man seeking to enhance his conversational prowess and social interactions. This book looks into the art of communication, offering a blend of practical advice, psychological insights, and real-world examples. It's tailored for those who wish to become more engaging, charismatic, and influential in both their personal and professional lives.

At its core, the book focuses on developing a well-rounded set of interests, honing storytelling skills, and mastering the nuances of personal engagement. It emphasizes the importance of being relatable, utilizing complimentary cold reading, and striking a balance between emotion and logic in conversations. The guide also provides strategies for using open-ended questions effectively, speaking your mind authentically, and the crucial role of active listening.

This book is not just another how-to book; it's a whole tool towards becoming a more confident, articulate, and socially adept individual in our modern world. By transforming the reader's approach to conversations, turning everyday interactions into meaningful connections. Whether it's in a business meeting, a social gathering, or a casual chat, this book equips its readers with the tools to captivate, connect, and communicate with confidence and ease.

The ultimate goal of "The Masculine Club" is to empower readers to take control of their interactions and leave a lasting impression. It's perfect for anyone looking to elevate their communication skills, build stronger relationships, and navigate the social world with a newfound sense of assurance and charisma.

And then there's emotional resilience. Gone are the days when men were expected to be unfeeling pillars of stoicism.

Today's masculinity embraces emotional intelligence. It's about being aware of one's emotions and handling them responsibly. Isn't it true that being emotionally resilient and empathetic makes for healthier, more fulfilling relationships, especially with women who often value emotional connection?

Don't forget, it is also important to remember that a strong masculine drive is not about overpowering or overshadowing others. It's about complementing and respecting. In interactions with women, it's not about asserting dominance, but about showing respect, understanding, and equality. Isn't a relationship, after all, a partnership where both individuals support and uplift each other?

Prepare to take the world by storm with this masterpiece.

Chapter1: The Renaissance Man's Playground

Develop A Wide Range of Interests.

"You don't have to know a TON about any given topic, just have a well-rounded set of interests.

This helps you relate to a wide variety of people."

Imagine this: a gentleman who can effortlessly switch from discussing the latest advancements in technology to passionately debating the merits of classic literature. This chapter is your guide to becoming that versatile individual who navigates through diverse conversations, connecting with people from all backgrounds.

Engage in the Diversity of Knowledge:

It's not about being an expert in everything; it's about being genuinely curious about the vast array of human knowledge. From science to the arts, from philosophy to pop culture, our Masculine Club member appreciates that each area contributes to the rich mosaic of life. We encourage you to sample various subjects, sparking not only intellectual growth but also fostering an appreciation for the expanse of human experience.

The Social Alchemist:

Ever found yourself at a social gathering where conversations ranged from quantum physics to the latest fashion trends? Our Renaissance Man not only survives but flourishes in such scenarios. By developing a diverse set of interests, you become a social alchemist, effortlessly transforming awkward silences into engaging dialogues. Whether you're networking at a business event or enjoying a casual dinner party, your ability to relate to a variety of people becomes a superpower.

Bridging the Generation Gap:

"The Masculine Club" is a bridge between generations, capable of discussing classic movies with the older crowd and debating the latest viral trends with the younger generation. By cultivating a broad spectrum of interests, you become a timeless conversationalist, transcending age barriers and establishing connections that go beyond the surface.

Passion-Driven Versatility:

While breadth is essential, depth is not to be overlooked. Discover what truly ignites your passion and immerse yourself in those subjects. Whether it's mastering a musical instrument, understanding the nuances of coding, or becoming a connoisseur of fine wines, your unique passions add depth to your character, making you not just well-rounded but fascinatingly complex.

So, dear reader, as you embark on this journey with "The Masculine Club," remember that being a Renaissance man is not about knowing everything; it's about embracing the limitless possibilities of knowledge.

Chapter 2: The Art of Storytelling

Make sure you prepare ahead of time.

Prepare some stories regarding your work, your upbringing, places you've been to, events you've attended, and your interests.

In this chapter, I will guide you through the process of crafting and sharing captivating stories. Remember, a well-told story not only entertains but also connects and resonates with your audience, creating unforgettable moments.

The Storyteller's Toolkit:

Every member of The Masculine Club should have a collection of stories ready to share. These stories are like arrows in your quiver, each one unique and ready for the right moment. Consider stories about your career achievements, challenges you've overcome, your upbringing, travels, events you've attended, and your hobbies. The key is to select stories that are not only interesting but also reveal something about your character and values.

Crafting Your Narrative:

A good story is more than just a series of events; it's about the emotions, the lessons learned, and the journey. When preparing your stories, focus on creating a narrative arc. Begin with a compelling setup that hooks your audience, then lead them through the twists and turns of your tale, and finally, conclude with a satisfying resolution. Remember, it's the ups and downs, the conflicts, and resolutions that make a story truly engaging.

Authenticity and Relatability:

Your stories should be authentic; they should resonate with truth and sincerity. Authenticity breeds connection. When people feel that you are sharing a genuine part of yourself, they are more likely to engage and empathize with your experiences. Moreover, find ways to make your stories relatable. Even if your audience hasn't had the same experiences, they should be able to connect with the emotions and insights your story conveys.

Adapting to Your Audience:

A skilled storyteller in The Masculine Club knows how to tailor their stories to their audience. The story you tell at a business conference might differ from the one you share at a casual gathering with friends. Pay attention to your audience's reactions and adjust your delivery accordingly. The goal is to captivate, whether it's through humor, suspense, or heartfelt moments.

Practice Makes Perfect:

Like any other skill, storytelling improves with practice. Rehearse your stories, refine them, and be open to feedback. You'll find that as you become more comfortable with storytelling, it becomes a natural and enjoyable part of your interactions.

Your stories should not be just mere narratives; they should act as bridges that connect you to others, revealing the depth and richness of your life experiences. So gather your tales, polish them with care, and be ready to share. As a member of The "Masculine Club", your stories are not just spoken words; they are the keys to building lasting connections and leaving a memorable impression.

Imagine you're at a sophisticated dinner party, a diverse gathering of individuals from various professional and cultural backgrounds. The room is abuzz with conversations, laughter, and the clinking of glasses. You, a distinguished member of The Masculine Club, find yourself amidst a small group, a blend of seasoned professionals and young, enthusiastic entrepreneurs.

As the conversation ebbs and flows, an opportunity presents itself in the chatter, a moment ripe for storytelling isn't it? You sense the audience's readiness for something engaging, something that will stir their minds and emotions.

You lean in slightly, ensuring you have everyone's attention, and begin your tale. It's a story about a challenge you faced during a mountain climbing expedition, a situation where you were tested both physically and mentally. Your voice, calm yet impassioned, draws your audience in, as you describe the steep, treacherous paths and the biting cold winds.

But your story isn't just about the climb; it's a metaphor for resilience and teamwork. You weave in moments where you had to rely on your companions, highlighting the value of trust and cooperation. The danger you faced isn't just a physical one, but also an emotional journey of overcoming self-doubt and fear.

As you approach the climax the moment you reached the summit your audience is visibly moved, hanging on to every word. You describe the exhilarating feeling of accomplishment, the breathtaking view, a symbol of what one can achieve through perseverance and collaboration.

Then, you masterfully tie it back to the present, to the very essence of the gathering. You talk about how, like mountain climbing, the path to success in any field is fraught with challenges, but with determination, support, and belief in oneself, any peak can be conquered.

Your story concludes, leaving a moment of reflective silence, followed by an outburst of applause and admiration. You've not only entertained your audience but also connected with them on a deeper level, imparting wisdom and inspiration.

In this scenario, your storytelling has achieved multiple objectives:

1. **Engagement**: You captivated your audience with a narrative that was both exciting and emotionally charged.

2. **Relatability**: By talking about universal themes like resilience and teamwork, you've connected with your audience regardless of their individual experiences.

3. **Inspiration**: Your story served as a source of motivation, encouraging others to face

their challenges with courage and optimism.

As a masculine figure, your storytelling skills should showcase your experiences and it is a sure way to win in the crows when the opportunity arises.

I was at a networking event last week, mingling with a diverse group of professionals. Amidst the usual exchange of pleasantries and business cards, I found myself in conversation with a woman named Sarah, who mentioned she worked in renewable energy.

I saw an opportunity to go beyond the surface. So, I asked her, "What do you like most about your job in renewable energy?" Her eyes lit up instantly. She began sharing not just the details of her job, but her passion for making a difference in the world. It was fascinating to hear her speak so enthusiastically.

As the conversation progressed, I took it a step further. "Why did you choose this field of work?" I inquired. This question opened a window into her personal journey. She recounted her childhood, how she grew up in a small town plagued by pollution, and how that inspired her to pursue a career in environmental conservation. It was a story of inspiration, driven by personal experiences and a deep sense of purpose. next time use this approach when you have a convo with anyone.

Feeling the conversation was going well, I ventured into a more reflective query, "If you could do any kind of work, without any constraints, what would you do?" Sarah paused thoughtfully, then shared her dream of starting an NGO focused on environmental education for children. This dream revealed her deeper aspirations and gave me a glimpse into her idealistic vision of the future.

Throughout our conversation, I made sure to listen actively, nodding and responding appropriately to show my genuine interest. I noticed how our interaction transitioned from a formal exchange to a more personal and engaging dialogue. We moved from discussing mere professional details to sharing values, dreams, and inspirations.

By the end of the conversation I had established a connection based on mutual understanding and respect. It was a clear demonstration of how personal, yet thoughtful questions can transform an ordinary chat into a meaningful interaction, creating a bond that goes beyond mere professional networking.

This experience was a testament to the principles of outlined above and how they can be effectively applied in real-life scenarios to build deeper, more substantial connections with those around us.

Chapter 4: Connecting Through Common Interests

Be More Relatable.

Explore mutual interests as much as you can. When you know how to relate to people, you'll be able to bond with them very quickly.

Isn't it amazing how shared passions can bridge the gap between strangers? Imagine walking into a room, feeling a bit out of place, and then you overhear someone mention your favorite book, sport, or even a hobby you're passionate about. Doesn't that instantly light up a spark of excitement within you?

You see, when we share a part of ourselves through our interests, we're not just talking about hobbies or preferences; we're sharing a piece of our identity. But how do you find that common ground, especially when it's not immediately obvious?

First, it's about being open and expressive about your own interests. Have you ever held back from mentioning your love for classical music or your weekend hiking adventures, worrying it might not be 'cool' enough? Well, guess what? Owning your interests with confidence can actually draw people towards you. People are attracted to passion and authenticity.

Who knows, your enthusiasm for birdwatching might just ignite a long, fascinating conversation with someone who shares the same passion or piques the interest of someone who's never considered it before.

Then there's the art of being curious. How often do we truly listen to understand, rather than just to respond? When you meet someone new, do you find yourself genuinely curious about their hobbies and passions? Asking questions about their interests isn't just polite small talk it's a doorway to a deeper understanding of who they are. And isn't it a thrilling moment when you discover a shared interest, no matter how niche it might be?

But what about those times when your interests don't align? Well, isn't that an opportunity in itself to learn something new? Imagine the possibilities when you open yourself up to understanding someone else's world. Could it be that your next favorite book, movie, or even a life-changing hobby is just one conversation away?

In "Connecting Through Common Interests," we delve into these dynamics, offering practical tips and real-life scenarios that demonstrate the power of shared passions in building connections. Whether it's in a professional setting, a social gathering, or even in the queue at your local coffee shop, finding and sharing common interests can transform ordinary interactions into extraordinary connections. It is time to explore the incredible potential of what you love and how it can connect you to the world around you? In this book, "The Masculine Club," one of the most important skills to master is how to be relatable. This chapter focuses on the simple yet effective method of connecting with others by finding and discussing shared interests. It's about using these common interests to make conversations more interesting and build stronger relationships quickly.

To be relatable, start by finding something in common with the person you are talking to. This could be anything - a hobby, a type of music, a favorite sport. For example, imagine you are at a neighborhood barbecue and you start talking to someone about hiking. You both love hiking. This common interest becomes a way for you to connect. You can share your favorite hiking trails, talk about hikes you've done, and maybe even plan to go hiking together. This shared interest creates a bond between you.

Once you find a shared interest, the next step is to talk more about it. Share your experiences and ask them about theirs. Show that you are really interested. For instance, if you meet someone at a photography exhibit and you both like the same kind of photography, you can talk more about it. Discuss different photographers you like, talk about your own photography, and share stories. This makes your conversation more engaging and helps you connect on a deeper level.

Being relatable also means being open to new things. If you're at a book club and someone talks about a book genre you don't know much about, show interest. Ask them for recommendations. This shows that you value their opinion and are open to learning about new things.

These shared interests do more than just make one conversation interesting. They often lead to more opportunities to socialize. For example, the person you met at the barbecue and talked about hiking with might invite you to join a hiking group. This expands your social circle and helps you meet more people who share your interests.

Finding and talking about shared interests is a key way to be more relatable. It makes conversations more enjoyable and helps build strong connections quickly. This chapter in "The Masculine Club" shows that by focusing on shared interests, you can turn simple chats into meaningful relationships and expand your social network. It's about connecting with others through the things you both enjoy and are passionate about.

Chapter 5: The Art of Complimentary Cold Reading

The three-step method of complimentary cold reading

Note: *Everyone appreciates a good compliment that feels personal.*

This part underlines the importance of such interpersonal skills in building strong, positive connections in both personal and professional realms. By mastering this art, you enhance your ability to connect with others in a meaningful and respectful way.

The concept of complimentary cold reading emerges as a nuanced and effective tool in the art of social interaction. This technique, when executed with sincerity and observation, can serve as a bridge to foster immediate rapport and establish a positive connection with someone, especially in initial encounters. This method involves giving a compliment that feels personal and genuine, helping to create an instant connection with someone you've just met. Here's how to effectively employ this technique:

Complimentary cold reading is a three-step process that begins with a keen observation, transitions into a personalized compliment, and culminates in associating the observed trait with a positive characteristic. This approach, however, goes beyond mere flattery; it involves a genuine recognition and appreciation of the unique aspects of an individual, which often go unnoticed.

The first step in complimentary cold reading is observation. This is where attention to detail plays a crucial role. In every interaction, there's an opportunity to notice something distinctive about a person it could be their attire, the way they articulate their thoughts, their laugh, or even something as subtle as their choice of accessories.

The objective here is to find something that genuinely stands out about the person. This step is critical because it lays the foundation for a compliment that doesn't just sound pleasant but feels meaningful to the recipient.

Moving to the second step, the compliment, the key is to ensure that it is both genuine and specific. Generic compliments often fail to resonate because they lack a personal touch. A well-crafted compliment based on the initial observation can instantly warm up the conversation and make the other person feel seen and appreciated. For instance, commenting on someone's unique sense of style in a way that highlights their individuality can be more impactful than a simple, "You look nice today."

The final and most crucial step is connecting the compliment to a positive trait or characteristic. This is what truly sets complimentary cold reading apart from ordinary flattery. By associating the observed quality with a deeper attribute, the compliment becomes more than just a comment on superficial qualities; it becomes a recognition of the person's character or values. For example, praising someone's meticulous work on a project and linking it to their dedication and attention to detail elevates the compliment to a testament of their work ethic and professionalism.

The effectiveness of complimentary cold reading lies in its ability to create an immediate and genuine connection. Using this three-step method of complimentary cold reading can help you make a memorable first impression.

It demonstrates your attentiveness, thoughtfulness, and ability to recognize and appreciate what makes others unique. In a world where surface-level interactions are common, taking the time to observe and articulate thoughtful compliments can be a powerful way to engage with others. It demonstrates empathy, attentiveness, and a genuine interest in the person.

The three-step method of complimentary cold reading

Step 1: Observe a Distinctive Feature or Quality

Step 2: Compliment Them on That Quality

Step 3: Relate It to a Positive Trait

Chapter 6: Beyond Logic – Embracing Emotional Connection

Stop Being So Logical.

<hr>

If you want to become an engaging conversationalist, you need to stop being so logical all the time.

One key aspect that often goes unnoticed is the importance of stepping beyond the edge of pure logic. Have you ever found yourself in a conversation that felt more like a lecture than a pleasant exchange? Or perhaps you've been on the receiving end of a chat that was all facts and no heart?

The truth is, while logical thinking and factual information are important, they aren't always the ingredients for a captivating conversation. Think about it: when was the last time a story filled with only statistics or technical details truly moved you? Emotions are the universal language that everyone understands and connects with. They add color, warmth, and relatability to our interactions.

So, how do you strike that balance between being informative and emotionally engaging? It starts with recognizing that not every conversation has to be a problem-solving session. Sometimes, people just want to share their experiences, feelings, or day-to-day stories. They aren't looking for solutions or in-depth analysis; they're seeking connection, empathy, and understanding. Firstly, self-awareness forms the foundation of emotional connection. It involves a deep and analytical understanding of one's emotional landscape. By recognizing and regulating one's emotions, individuals can interact with others more empathetically and effectively. This self-regulation is an identification strategic approach to managing the male emotional landscape to facilitate constructive interactions.

Empathy is the second critical component. It differs from sympathy in its depth of understanding and emotional immersion. Empathy requires an individual to intellectually and emotionally place themselves in another's situation, understanding their emotions from their perspective. This empathic engagement is crucial for building trust and rapport.

Effective communication is the third pillar. It necessitates the articulation of one's emotions in a clear and constructive manner while actively listening and responding to the emotions of others. This bilateral emotional exchange is key to fostering understanding and a sense of connection.

Vulnerability, often misconstrued as a weakness, is actually a strategic tool in building emotional connections. It involves openly sharing emotions, fears, and aspirations, which invites others to engage at a deeper, more genuine level. Vulnerability breaks down barriers and fosters authentic connections.

Lastly, embracing emotional connection has a significant impact on conflict resolution. Analyzing conflicts through an emotional lens allows for a deeper understanding of the underlying issues. It promotes empathetic and harmonious resolutions, acknowledging that emotions are often at the heart of disagreements.

For instance, if a friend is talking about a challenging day at work, they might not be seeking a step-by-step guide to tackle their professional woes. More often than not, they're looking for a listening ear, someone who can understand and empathize with their situation. In such scenarios, responding with emotional intelligence maybe a simple, "That sounds really tough, how did you feel about it?" can be more impactful than a logical breakdown of what they should or shouldn't have done.

Moreover, breaking away from the shackles of logic can open doors to more creative and enjoyable conversations. Have you ever noticed how stories, jokes, and personal anecdotes often light up a room more than technical talk? It's because they allow us to share a piece of ourselves our experiences, our emotions, our humanity. They create a space where people can laugh, empathize, and connect on a deeper level.

In conclusion, while logic and facts have their place, they aren't the sole components of engaging conversations. To truly connect with others and be an engaging conversationalist, embracing the emotional aspect of communication is key. It's about understanding the power of empathy, the joy of shared laughter, and the beauty of simply being human. Remember, sometimes the heart needs to be heard more than the mind.

Chapter 7: The Power of Open-Ended Questions

Ask More Open-Ended Questions

Whatever you do, avoid asking closed-ended questions which can be answered with one word.

To improve the quality of your interactions, try asking more open-ended questions.

Have you ever found yourself in a conversation that fizzled out faster than a sparkler on the Fourth of July? Maybe it was filled with questions like "Did you have a good weekend?" only to receive a flat "Yes" in response. It's in moments like these that the magic of open-ended questions becomes evident.

We will continue by emphasizing on the importance of enhancing the quality of our interactions. One of the most effective ways to do this is by asking more open-ended questions. But why is this so crucial? Well, think about it: when was the last time a "Yes" or "No" answer led to an intriguing conversation?

Open-ended questions are the keys that unlock more engaging, deeper, and meaningful conversations. They encourage the person you're speaking with to share more than just the bare minimum. For example, instead of asking "Did you like the movie?", which can be answered with a simple "Yes" or "No," try "What did you think about the movie?" This type of question invites elaboration, opinions, feelings, and can lead to a more enriched conversation.

Moreover, open-ended questions demonstrate a genuine interest in the other person's thoughts and experiences. They send a message that you care about what they have to say and are interested in listening to them. This can be especially powerful in building relationships, whether personal or professional.

For instance, in a work setting, asking a colleague, "What challenges are you facing with your current project?" rather than "Is your project going well?" can provide insights into their experiences and pave the way for collaboration or support.

Furthermore, these questions can often lead to unexpected and exciting territories in a conversation. They open doors to stories, opinions, and ideas that might otherwise remain unexplored. Have you ever been pleasantly surprised by where a conversation went just because you asked the right question?

These questions are more than just conversation extenders; they are tools that facilitate deeper understanding, foster stronger connections, and enrich our interactions. So next time you find yourself in a conversation, remember: your power as a Masculine Club strategist is to unlock interesting dialogue may just lie in the question, "What's your story?"

Go ahead and make good use of it.

Chapter 8: The Art of Honest Expression

Practice saying what's on your mind.

* * *

When you start a conversation with someone new, you may feel like small talk is awkward and meaningless.

People will judge you for what you say as little as you walk around and judge others for what they say.

Have you ever been stuck in a conversation, dancing around safe topics like the weather or the latest sports scores, and thought to yourself, "Why can't I just say what's really on my mind?" Well, why not indeed? The importance of speaking your mind and how it can transform your conversations from mundane to genuinely engaging is what this chapter seeks to address.

Let's face it, initiating small talk with someone new can sometimes feel like a chore. But what if you shifted gears and started expressing your actual thoughts? Sure, it might seem risky. You might wonder, "What if they judge me for what I say?" But think about it do you spend your time judging every word others say? Probably not, right?

The practice of saying what's on your mind is about being authentic in your conversations. It's about moving past the superficial "Nice day, isn't it?" and venturing into more personal territory. Imagine starting a chat with, "I've been really into gardening lately. There's something about watching things grow that fascinates me. Do you have any hobbies that surprise you?" This approach can turn a standard exchange into a more interesting and meaningful conversation.

Now, you might be thinking, "What if my thoughts aren't interesting to the other person?" Well, never mind that. The key is in your delivery and enthusiasm. Sometimes, it's not about the topic but how you talk about it. Your passion can be infectious and may invite the other person to open up about their interests too.

Of course, this doesn't mean you should say every single thing that pops into your head without a filter. It's about being considerate and thoughtful in what you choose to share. For instance, if a thought comes up and you're unsure whether to share it, a quick mental check like, "Is this something that could lead to an interesting conversation?" can be helpful.

Imagine you're in your favorite coffee shop, standing in line, waiting to order your usual. There's a bit of a wait, and you notice the person in front of you is holding a book that you've recently read and loved. Normally, you might shy away from commenting, sticking to the safety of your own thoughts. But today, recalling the advice from "The Masculine Club," you decide to take a different approach.

You lean forward slightly and say, "I couldn't help but notice the book you're holding. 'The Alchemist,' right? I finished it last month, and it really made me think about my personal journey. What do you think about it so far?"

The person turns around, a bit surprised but with a smile, "Oh, this? I just started it, but it's been intriguing. What did you find most compelling about your personal journey?"

Just like that, you've broken the ice. Instead of a silent wait in line, you've now engaged in a meaningful conversation. You talk about the themes of the book, share a bit about your own experiences, and even touch upon other books and authors you enjoy. By the time you reach the counter to order, you've made a connection, all because you chose to share what was on your mind.

As you sip your coffee, you reflect on the interaction. It wasn't just about the book; it was about taking the risk to express your thoughts and interests openly. You realize that these genuine interactions are not only possible but also quite simple to initiate. It's a matter of stepping out of your comfort zone and into a space of authenticity.

This scenario exemplifies the essence of speaking your mind. It shows that by sharing your genuine thoughts and interests, you can turn ordinary moments into opportunities for connection and discovery. It's about breaking free from the constraints of 'safe' conversation and embracing the authenticity of your thoughts.

It's about finding the courage to be yourself and to share your thoughts and interests openly. Remember, speaking your mind is not just about making conversation; it's about making genuine connections. The next time you find yourself in a chat, think about dropping the usual script and sharing something real. You might be surprised at how rewarding an honest conversation can be. After all, isn't a genuine connection what we're all looking for?

Chapter 9: The Attentive Listening Technique

Sometimes, all we can think about is if we come off as weird if we're blushing or if our heart is about to jump out of our chest.

The key is to calm your mind by focusing intensively on what the other person is saying.

The Attentive Listening Technique is a skill that transforms conversations, fosters deeper connections, and promotes a genuine understanding between individuals. Now, have you ever wondered why some conversations leave you feeling genuinely understood, while others feel superficial? The secret ingredient often lies in the art of listening, not just hearing.

At its core, Attentive Listening is about being fully present in a conversation. It's more than just a passive act of receiving sound; it's an active process of engagement with the speaker. This technique involves several key elements, each playing an important role in making the listener not just a participant but an active contributor to the conversation.

Firstly, there's the aspect of nonverbal communication. Are you aware of how your body language can speak volumes about your level of engagement? Maintaining eye contact, nodding, and leaning slightly forward are nonverbal cues that signal to the speaker that you are fully engaged. But, is it just about your body language? No, it's also about recognizing and responding to the speaker's nonverbal cues, which can often convey more than their words.

Secondly, the technique emphasizes the importance of reflective listening. This involves paraphrasing or summarizing what the speaker has said to confirm understanding. It's not just about repeating their words; it's about showing that you've processed and understood their message.

Another critical aspect is avoiding interruptions. How often do we jump in with our own stories or advice, cutting off the speaker? Attentive Listening requires patience, allowing the speaker to express their thoughts fully without interjections. It's about creating a safe space where the speaker feels heard and valued.

The technique also involves asking open-ended questions. These questions encourage the speaker to elaborate and provide more depth to their thoughts. But remember, the aim is not to steer the conversation but to deepen your understanding of the speaker's perspective.

Finally, there's the emotional aspect of listening. Attentive Listening means being empathetic, acknowledging the speaker's emotions, and responding appropriately. It's about connecting with the speaker on an emotional level, which fosters trust and a stronger bond.

Incorporating the Attentive Listening Technique into your conversations can have a profound impact. It enhances relationships, fosters mutual respect, and promotes a deeper understanding of others. Isn't it remarkable how such a simple shift in our listening approach can lead to more meaningful and fulfilling interactions? So, the next time you find yourself in a conversation, ask yourself: Am I just hearing, or am I attentively listening?

It's a common scenario, where our minds race with thoughts like, "Do I sound weird?" or "Am I blushing right now?" in convos, there's a simple yet effective key to overcoming this: *focus intently on what the other person is saying.*

The significance of being present in conversations. When you truly listen to someone, it's not just about hearing their words; it's about understanding their thoughts, feelings, and perspectives. It's a skill that requires practice and mindfulness, but the rewards are immense.

Imagine you're in a discussion and your mind starts to wander. You begin to worry about how you're coming across. Are you speaking too much? Too little? Instead of spiraling into these thoughts, redirect your focus back to the speaker.

What are they really trying to convey? What's the emotion behind their words? This shift in attention not only calms your anxious thoughts but also enriches the conversation.

Now, you might think, "But what if I'm just not that interested in what they're saying?" Well, never mind that for a moment. The act of listening attentively can turn even mundane topics into something more engaging. You start to notice nuances in the conversation that you would have missed otherwise. And who knows, you might find yourself intrigued by a subject you initially thought was dull.

Remember, people can usually tell when you're genuinely interested in what they have to say. It shows in your body language, your responses, and your overall demeanor. By focusing on the conversation, you not only ease your own anxieties but also create a space where the other person feels heard and valued.

In conclusion, this chapter is a reminder that the essence of good conversation lies in how well we listen, not just in what or how we speak. It's about being fully present and engaged with the person you're talking to. So next time you find yourself getting lost in your head during a conversation, remember: the key to a meaningful interaction is right there in front of you, waiting to be heard.

Chapter 10: Final Thoughts

After reading this book, one must understand that when we talk about masculinity today, it's clear that the old rulebook has been tossed out. It's no longer just about being the strongest or the loudest in the room. In this era, standing out as a man is more about how you carry yourself, especially in conversations. Let's get into the nuts and bolts of how a modern man can demonstrate masculinity through the art of conversation.

First off, it's crucial to understand that true masculinity in conversation isn't about dominating the dialogue. It's about balance. The modern man knows when to speak and when to listen. He understands that a good conversation is like a dance it's a two-way street. Studies have shown that individuals who engage in active listening are perceived as more trustworthy and empathetic. This perception is a cornerstone of modern masculinity.

Then there's the content of what you're saying. Gone are the days when men were expected to talk only about a limited range of 'masculine' topics. Today, a man who can comfortably chat about a variety of subjects is not only more interesting but also shows he's connected to the world around him. According to a Harvard study, diversifying your interests and knowledge makes you more appealing and engaging in social situations.

Emotional intelligence plays a massive role here. It's about being tuned into the emotional undercurrents of a conversation. A masculine figure today is someone who can sense discomfort, acknowledge it, and steer the conversation in a direction that makes everyone feel at ease. This ability is a true demonstration of strength and control, more so than any display of physical power.

Now, think about the tone and style of your conversation. Masculinity today is about confidence, not arrogance. There's a fine line between the two. A confident man can state his opinions without belittling others. He's open to other viewpoints and can engage in healthy debate without turning it into a conflict. This approach not only shows maturity but also respect for others, traits that are highly valued in any social setting.

Humor is another key aspect. A well-timed joke or a light-hearted comment can ease tensions and show a side of you that is relatable and human. However, it's important to be mindful of the type of humor used. Insensitive or offensive jokes are a big no-no. They can do more harm than good, not only to your image but also to the comfort of those around you.

Lastly, let's talk about authenticity. In a world full of facades, being genuine is a breath of fresh air. Authenticity in your conversations demonstrates a comfortable sense of self, a trait that is inherently masculine. It's about being true to your beliefs and values, and expressing them in a way that's respectful and considerate of others.

In conclusion, modern masculinity can be demonstrated through conversation which makes use of tecniques such as active listening, emotional intelligence, diverse knowledge, confidence, humor, and authenticity. It's about being strong yet sensitive, knowledgeable yet open-minded, confident yet humble. Mastering this art not only sets you apart but also earns you respect and admiration in any circle. So, the next time you're in a conversation, remember, it's not just about what you say, but how you say it and how well you listen. That's the mark of a truly modern, masculine man.

In "The Masculine Club," we emphasize the significance of being present in conversations. When you truly listen to someone, it's not just about hearing their words; it's about understanding their thoughts, feelings, and perspectives. It's a skill that requires practice and mindfulness, but the rewards are immense.

Imagine you're in a discussion and your mind starts to wander. You begin to worry about how you're coming across. Are you speaking too much? Too little? Instead of spiraling into these thoughts, redirect your focus back to the speaker. What are they really trying to convey? What's the emotion behind their words? This shift in attention not only calms your anxious thoughts but also enriches the conversation.

Now, you might think, "But what if I'm just not that interested in what they're saying?" Well, never mind that for a moment. The act of listening attentively can turn even mundane topics into something more engaging. You start to notice nuances in the conversation that you would have missed otherwise. And who knows, you might find yourself intrigued by a subject you initially thought was dull.

Remember, people can usually tell when you're genuinely interested in what they have to say. It shows in your body language, your responses, and your overall demeanor. By focusing on the conversation, you not only ease your own anxieties but also create a space where the other person feels heard and valued.

As we draw to a close on the subject of mastering the art of conversation as a masculine figure, let's consolidate our final thoughts. Throughout "The Masculine Club," we've journeyed through various facets that transform ordinary interactions into captivating exchanges. It's not just about what you say, but how you say it, and the underlying understanding and empathy you bring to each conversation.

First and foremost, the breadth of your interests sets the stage. Having a wide range of topics at your disposal is like having a key to different worlds. Each conversation is an opportunity to open a new door, to explore and connect. Isn't it remarkable how a single, well-placed comment about a shared interest can turn a stranger into an acquaintance, or even a friend?

Then, there's the art of storytelling. Our lives are tapestries of experiences, and sharing these stories not only captivates but also builds bridges. Each anecdote you share paints a picture of who you are, inviting others to do the same. Isn't it through these shared narratives that we find common ground?

Personal engagement, the cornerstone of any meaningful interaction, cannot be overstated. Asking thoughtful, open-ended questions shows a genuine interest in others. It's about delving deeper than the superficial layers of small talk. Isn't true connection found in the depths, rather than the surface?

Being relatable and approachable is the thread that ties all these aspects together. When you find common ground with someone, you create a sense of camaraderie and comfort. It's about recognizing the shared human experience in each of us.

Lastly, remember the balance between logic and emotion. A conversation is not just an exchange of information but a dance of personalities, emotions, and ideas. A well-timed compliment, an empathetic ear, and the courage to speak your mind all contribute to your allure as a conversationalist.

Key Takeaways

1. Develop a Wide Range of Interests: Cultivate knowledge in various fields to connect with a diverse audience. This versatility makes conversations more engaging and allows you to relate to different people.

2. Storytelling Skills: Harness the power of personal stories. Sharing experiences from work, travel, or hobbies makes conversations more personal and memorable.

3. Personal Engagement: Ask open-ended, slightly personal questions. This approach transforms basic interactions into meaningful exchanges, showing genuine interest in others.

4. **Relatability:** Find common ground to establish a quick and strong connection. Sharing mutual interests or experiences can significantly deepen your interactions.

5. **Complimentary Cold Reading**: Offer genuine compliments based on observable traits or behaviors. This can create a positive and memorable impression, opening doors to deeper conversations.

6. **Balance Emotion and Logic**: Engage in conversations with a blend of emotional intelligence and logical thought. This balance makes interactions more dynamic and appealing.

7. **Use Open-Ended Questions**: Steer away from yes-or-no questions. Instead, ask open-ended questions that encourage detailed responses and foster a richer dialogue.

8. **Speak Your Mind:** Share your thoughts and opinions openly. Authenticity in conversations builds trust and makes you more relatable.

9. **Focus on the Conversation**: Pay close attention to what the other person is saying. Active listening demonstrates respect and interest, making the other person feel valued.

10. **Avoid Over-Logic in Conversations:** Understand that conversations are not just about exchanging facts; they're about connecting on a human level. Balance logical discussions with emotional and personal elements.

OTHER BOOKS BY THE AUTHOR

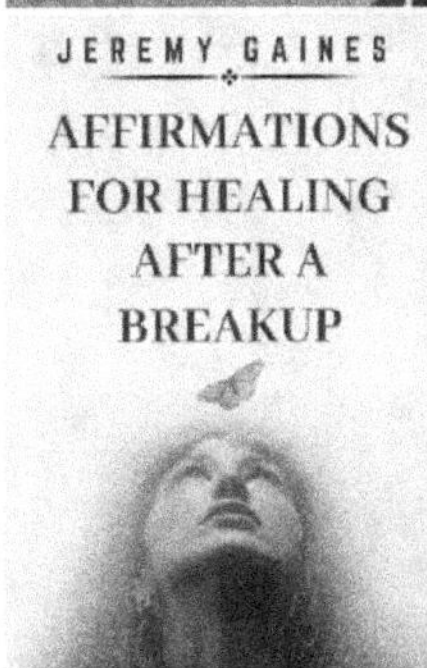

Get all on Amazon